Art is the Best Revenge

The Poetic Deviance of Jim Larsen

by JimLarsen

This book is dedicated to Samantha.

The Coward Who Ran
(A Kalani Story)

I'm the coward who ran.
My belly is fat
and my skin is tan.
I'm terrified of danger
and avoid it
when I can.
Just call me
The Coward who ran.

When the earthquake shook
6.9
I said,
Gotta save this ass of mine.
You guys are on your own
I need to go.
Where am I going?
I don't know.
Run through the Glass Door
because I'm feeling low.
The Eagle has landed,
it is so.

I gotta go
I gotta go!
Gotta escape this lava flow.
It's coming at me,
it's quite a show.
I'll just leave behind
a giant mess.
You guys will clean it up,
uhm, right?
Yeah, I guess.

Accountability
is so over-rated
so I'll be the guy
who's forever hated
for instilling fear,

and white guilt
for a community
that's gated.
aAd never you mind
that I'm obligated
to lead you
through times of change.
But you know what?
I'm in over my head.
This is beyond my range.
I don't know what I'm doing.
I haven't a clue.
But I can't look weak
in front of you.
So I'll find an excuse.
Ah! Here's one that works.
The lava is flowing,
and you guys are jerks!
So I'll run now
watch me go.
Don't want to get trapped
in this lava flow.

So you'll understand
if I don't look back.
You guys can handle it.
Cover my tracks.
Come on my little rabbit friend,
it's not our fault
this all came to an end.
The founder did it.
He did it all!
It's all because of him
this place had its downfall.

If I say it enough
people will start
to believe it's true.
It worked with them;
it's working with you.
Now let's get out of here
before they realize the truth,
that I'm a clueless dick
and they uncover the proof.
Run! Run! Run!
Run through the Glass Door
Never look back.
The Eagle has landed
just abandon the shack.

The Eagle has landed
I'm the coward who ran.
My eyes are dark
and my skin is tan.
Times got tough
and I'm not a fan
of being in over my head.
So I'm the coward who ran.

Lied to About a Rainbow

Ever been lied to about a rainbow? I have. Now, the question you should be asking right now is, Jim? How did that make you feel? I'd like to tell you it made me feel sad or it made me feel angry, because I understand those feelings. But those aren't the words. I was lied to about a rainbow, and that made me feel small.

You said there was a rainbow! You pointed to it in the sky! And I got excited! I believed you, man! I thought you were my friend, but no. You ain't no friend of mine. I thought, "All right! A rainbow!" But when I looked, it wasn't there. There wasn't anythiI wonder how many people are like me when hugging. That's the problem. If I'm hugging somebody, I can't see their face, so I don't know if they are rolling their eyes and making weird faces. It is probably a safe bet that they are, so that's what I do too just to get back at them for doing that.
ng. Nothing.

You are a liar! Lie about your age! Lie about virginity! You can even lie about your prison tattoos! Believe me, I've heard them all! But you son of a bitch! You lied to me about a rainbow!

Rainbows are filled with magic and fantasy. Oh! There's a pot of gold at the end of the rainbow! Look! Spritely elves are dancing a lively jig while that unicorn flies off to the moon! Aren't rainbows wonderful! Sure they are, when they are real. There is no magic in a lied about rainbow though. Why would you do that? You are a sick, sick, bastard who just fucked their own karma up beyond redemption.

You know what's going to happen? I know it already. I do. In your next incarnation, you're going to be unicorn. But you know what? Your wings are going to be broken and you're not going to be able to fly over all the rainbows like your unicorn friends, that's if you have any friends, which you might not because liars don't deserve friends. And there I'll be no matter what, in every life. I'll incarnate as a mighty, mighty man with fourteen billion dollars in the bank and a nice watch and a cool car that goes super-fast and I'll have a beautiful wife who loves me for real and won't ever leave me, because she loves me, and I'll see you, and I'll say, "Ah. Look at that poor unicorn with its broken wings. Poor little guy. He can't even fly over the rainbow. Poor, poor unicorn."

And I'll be compassionate, because I'm always compassionate e time I've lived. So I'll hand feed you some Kalani made granola, and some skittles, and some marshmallows, or whatever, and you'll be really happy and your happiness will make me happy, so we will be happy together. Then I'll scratch you at that sweet spot on your back just above your tail that makes animals go "Ah yeah... don't stop, don't stop, don't stop, hey why'd you stop?" It's going to be a beautiful, magical moment made all the sweeter by the spirit and bond of friendship between us.

Then, I'm going to kick you hard right in the ass and I'm going to say to you, "Hey! Remember that time you lied to me about that rainbow? Now you know how it made me feel. I hope you remember that, but if you forget, don't worry. I'll be back to remind you."

So, the moral here is, don't lie to me about rainbows. If there's not a rainbow in the sky, don't say there is. It's a stupid thing to lie about and only stupid people tell lies like that. Are you stupid? Are you? I don't think so, but maybe you are. Obviously. Obviously stupid... because only stupid people lie about rainbows.

Change the World

You cannot change the world. You can only change your thoughts of the world. By changing your thoughts, you change the world. Forget what said about not being able to change the world, because actually you can.

Careful What You Say

There are those certain things that you are only allowed to think, but never say out loud, because if you say them out loud, you run the risk of losing friends or getting into trouble, maybe even punched. An example of this is, say you have this particular group of friends, and then one day one of these friends gets deported and has to go back their own country, like Canada, maybe. Here, you have to say things like, "Aww man! That sucks. That's terrible that you have to go back. We're going to miss you. Hope you make it back soon!" That's what you have to say no matter what, even if what you really want to say is more like, "Well that sucks, but in a way I'm glad because you were always kind of annoying. I'm going to enjoy the peace of not having you around. I hope the best for you, but in a way, I hope they don't let you back in the country." Try saying that though, and see if you don't get into trouble over it. And here now too, you are expected to say a few things about what a great person so and so is, so you better think of something. You don't want to be the one person in the crowd not showing sympathy for the deported guy.

Serving in the Kitchen

I work in the kitchen of the intentional community where I live, and it's my job to serve food. Sometimes, somebody will come through the line that I don't like and I feel like I am compromising myself by having to serve them. Every time I put food on their plate, I feel a piece of my soul slipping away.

To be honest, there are only two people who give me that feeling, and they have no idea who they are; I am good at keeping a poker face. One is a boy, and the other is a girl, but I'm not saying who they are. You may have a theory about it, but probably, the answer will surprise you. You may even be saying to yourself, "I bet he's talking about me." To which I can only say, "Yeah. Maybe." Or it could be the person to the left of you. Or it could be the person to the right of you. You just don't know, do you? No. You don't. And you never will because I will never say, except for maybe when I am on my death bed

Yeah, that's what I'll do. this will be my death bed confession. My last words will be, "I never liked it when I had to serve…" and then I'll whisper it, almost inaudibly except for whoever that one person will be who is bent over with their ear close to my mouth to catch my final words.
That person will gasp in shock, maybe even in horror as they stand to face the crowd that has gathered in the room. This person's face will be pale, their body trembling and they will say, "He never liked to serve… and then they will say the names of the people I don't like to serve in the kitch-en.

The collective shock of the crowd will be palpable as the entire paradigm that they had all built the foundation of their lives on shifts. Now they must now see me, Jim Larsen, the son of William and Joan, in a completely new context and light that they never before had to consider.

But none of that is going to happen for awhile, so don't worry too much about it for the time being. Just come on through the line. Tell me what you want on your plate, and I'll put it there for you so you can go on your way and eat your meal. Don't worry about me. I'll be fine.

Leilani Estate

Leilani Estate,
I still think you're great,
although you're covered in lava.

Leilani, Leilani,
you're so close to Kalani,
Let's meet at Uncle Robert's for some Kava.

Leaving

I'm leaving now
I'm leaving soon.
I'm getting on a train that leaves at noon.
I'm going to go across this land.
I'm going to sing my songs in a country band.

Yodel lay-hee
Yodel lay-hee
Yodel lay-hee-hoo- ha-hoo

I'll see you in Denver
I'll see you in Main
Grab your passport
And I'll see you in Spain.
I'll see you Zurich
I'll see you in France
You're gonna fall in love
On the night of the Dance.

Yodel lay-hee-hoo-ha-hoo-ha-hoo-hoo-hoo
Yodel lay-hee
Yodel lay-hee
Yodel Lay-hee-hoo

Gonna go
Gotta go
Here I go
Where do I go?
Oh, I don't know.
Just gonna get on a train
That goes across this land
And try to find some players
For my country band.

Yodel lay-hee
Yodel lay-hee, Yodel Lay-hee-hoo

11

World's Best Job

I hear this announcement all the time at airports: "All unattended baggage may be damaged or destroyed." That's gotta be one of the coolest jobs in the world- being the guy who gets to damage or destroy unattended baggage.

I can imagine it, TSA dudes dragging unattended baggage out onto the tarmac, kicking it, lifting it over their heads and throwing it down with the brute force of a 600 pound gorilla, yawlping with unabandoned enthusiasm as they whomp on it with baseball bats wrapped in barbed wire. They probably have a fire barrel, because it can get cold out there on the tarmac. Fire barrels are awesome. Eventually, you know somebody's going to bring out some M-80s and light those suckers up and toss them on the bag to watch it explode. That's gotta be rewarding.

That's the job I really want. Seriously, who do I send my resume to? Because I can't take another day of processing Freedom of Information Act requests for the government in this damn cubicle. My boss gets too jittery when I roll in my fire barrel.

A Bad Day at Kalani

They say Kalani is "Heaven on Earth" and probably it is. But even in Heaven, you sometimes have a bad day. Obviously.

A Few days ago was pretty much the worst day of my life ever. You see, I am an early riser, so I like to go to the lanai and drink coffee and write in my journal before it gets crowded. So the other day, I did that, and I was hungry for an English muffin, and guess what happened! As I was tearing the two halves of the muffin apart, the bottom part got all messed up and a big chunk of it was stuck to the top part, so it was all out of whack and uneven. I wanted to put it back in the bag and start over with a new one, but I don't want to be "that" guy. So I go ahead and run it through the toaster anyway, and guess what! It didn't even get brown! Not even a little bit! What kind of bullshit toaster is that? So I run it through a second time, and now it's burned! WTF!

And now it goes from bad to worse! I put butter on it, and I grab a jelly jar, and somebody left a bunch of butter inside the jar! And I'm like, "What's wrong with you people! Don't give me your sloppy butter seconds. God!" And then later I go through the breakfast line and I ask for some oatmeal. It's simple enough, right? The server puts the cup on the plate, they put the oatmeal in the cup. Right? I don't know the person's name, but do you know what he did? He got a big plop of oatmeal on the plate! Seriously! Right where my cheesy eggs are supposed to go! And then, to add insult to injury, he asks me, "What else would you like?" I said "I'd like a clean plate!" I guess to this guy thought it was just a joke, because he laughed at me like I was there only to amuse him. So I went ahead and put up with oatmeally cheesy eggs even though I really didn't want to. Man!

And then later, I was walking on the path from the dining lanai to guest services and I saw somebody coming that I don't like. I mean, I really really really really really don't like this person, and I don't want to say "hi" or anything to them. This is somebody who, like a smoke detector to a nine volt battery, slowly drains my energy until I am but an empty shell, dead and depleted inside. This is somebody who uses their very presence as a weapon, knowing I don't like them, so they linger around me just to make me deal with them like a giant mosquito I would go to jail for swatting.

13

So I think, maybe I can just look down at the ground and walk by and I won't have to say anything. But guess what? They go and say "Hi" to me, so now I'm stuck having to say "Hi" back even though it kills me to do it. So I say, "Hi" flatly without any conviction or aloha in my tone or demeanor, all the while thinking, gosh, I wish you would die. Then I think, what if they announce at the Monday morning meeting that a coconut fell on their and they're dead? I think my first thought would be "Hmm." My second thought would be "Man! I love mango crisp! Wouldn't it be great if they had that for dessert tonight? "

And then later, I was walking up the path for lunch, and guess what happened? I pebble got stuck in my sandal! I'm like, "Oh my God, that did not just happen!" So I shake my foot trying to get it out, and it won't go! It's stuck in there, and it hurts! So I dig my finger under my foot trying to get at it, but all it does is push the pebble in farther where it's going to hurt even more. I was pretty much willing to give up on life after that, and why wouldn't I? But then I thought, after all I've been through today, things can only get better from here. There might even be mango crisp for dessert. I'd hate to miss out on that.

But things didn't get better. Things got as far away from better as they possibly could. Lunch was fine, but dinner sure wasn't. Not only did the server slop soup all over my plate, but there wasn't even any mango crisp for dessert! You know what they had for dessert? It was some ridiculous gluten free something or other. Whose idea was it to pander to these gluten free fanatics, anyway? I mean, come on! Live on the wild side and have some flour in your food. You do know, don't you, that the whole idea of gluten allergies is a hoax dreamed up by the Nature's Path Cookie Company to sell more of their tasteless brownies, and because you suckers fell for it, now we all have to suffer during dessert. Thanks. Thanks guys! Appreciate it! Needless to say, the evening got worse and worse and worse. Nothing good happened. Nothing good at all. I won't even tell you what I stepped in on the way to Hale Aloha or what got spilled on my shirt.

But I took the day for what it was- just that- a day. Not a bad life or even a bad week. Just a bad day. Even in paradise, a bad day happens once in a while. You just get through them. What else can you do? As Tom Hanks said in Castaway- "So now I know what I have to do. I have to keep breathing. And tomorrow the sun will rise, and who knows what the tide will bring in?" And the next day, the sun did rise and brought with it the possibility to transform this new day into much better day, and it was a much better day. We didn't have mango crisp for dessert, but at least it wasn't some silly gluten free crap, so how bad of a day could it have been?

Fat Naked Man Talk Story

Walked to Kehena Beach intent on a swim
but the waves were pretty bad
so I was afraid to go in.
I sat on the beach, enjoyed the beauty
of the sea.
Next thing I know, a fat naked man's in front of me.
He's lunging forward
making movements with his hands
I think it's Tai Chi.
I wish he wouldn't.

Makes me uncomfortable.
Out of my comfort zone.
Maybe I'll write something about it.
I hear they do open mic here.
I'll read it out loud.
Test the waters.
See if they like my style.
So I read what I wrote before I went home
but nobody knew what to think
of my first open mic poem

Do we laugh?
Do we cry?
Hey, who is that guy?
He's kind of quiet,
kind of shy.
Does he ever say "Hi?"

Raven liked it.
Maybe I wrote it for her.
We hit it off.
Became good friends.
She's really cool.
We explored the island together
in a rented jeep.

Made good memories
that I intend to keep.
Forever.

My first three months went by so fast
I was living a life
I wanted to last.
But it couldn't.
Had responsibilities.
Things to get back to.
All that kind of stuff.
You know the drill.

So I went back home
and back to my job
Had to wear a tie,
couldn't be a Punatic slob.
This wasn't me,
not anymore.
My heart's gone from it.
Didn't have any happiness.
I couldn't hear the coqui frogs.
I was miserable.
No pool to go for a swim
no conversations to get lost in.
I wasn't happy.

Home wasn't home
not anymore.
All my old friends had become such a bore.
My job wasn't what I wanted to do.
I wanted to be on the island
and get a tattoo.
I wanted to watch lava
flow to the sea.
I wanted to
Hang out with Raven
and drink kawa tea.

I wanted to read tarot cards.

And read poems for open mic
Practice Reiki
and go on a hike.
Make a movie
and then part two.
Maybe travel the world,
is what I wanted to do.
Not sit in traffic.
and ride a subway train.
I wanted to walk in the jungle
and dance in the rain.

I had to get back.
That's all I knew,
My spirited had expanded,
it really grew.
It was too big now for my old home,
it wasn't even with me,
it took off to roam.

It was back at Kehena,
the black sand beach.
It was looking to be inspired
where inspiration is always within reach.
It was splashing in the waves
and lying in the sand.
It wasn't native there,
but sure felt at home in this adopted land.

I finally made made it back
and Raven was there too.
The fat naked man had leaned kung-fu.
I liked my life
And my life life liked me.
I was back where I belonged,
there by the sea.
My second three months
soon became three years.
It was clear this where I needed to stay.
It's been eleven years

and I'm still there to this day.

It's a different island
with a different beach.
They gave me a job
so now I teach.
Middle schoolers.

But inspiration is still easy to find.
Once I get out of myself
And expand my mind.
See a few things
I've not seen before.
Get in a jeep and go explore.
I explore with others now
Raven's not here.
But I silently toast her
with each and every beer.
Fat Naked Man
Doing Tai Chi on the Beach,
Must you stand so close?

Fat Naked Man
Doing Tai Chi on the Beach,
Must you stand so close?
Fat Naked Man…

One Egg

Serve them
one egg,
one egg,
one egg no more!

Is this a budget cutback?

Yes, we're poor.
But don't tell them the truth,
tell them a lie!
Eggs are bad for you.
Eat more than one
and you will die.

Will they believe that?
They seem pretty smart.

Just tell them two are bad for their heart.

I don't think they are so naïve.

Ah! I got another trick up my sleeve.
Tell them this,
they are bound to believe.
Tell them all the eggs in the world
have been recalled.
People eating them are all going bald.
Eggs cause hair follicles to shrivel and die.
Just look at Jim Larsen
he's a bald guy.
He has no hair
and eats eggs everyday.

Now that's a really stupid
thing to say.
He's been bald since before you were born,

it's because he once married a Capricorn.
Capricorns were all conceived in Hell
marry one and things will happen
too terrible to tell.
They all have horns
and a cloven hoof;
you don't want to
have one under your roof.
A Capricorn is the the devil's plaything.
Jim made the mistake of giving one a wedding ring.

Okay, I get it.
I won't tell them that.
How about we say eggs will make you fat.

Still kind of dumb
but if you're opposed to the truth
you could say that's what happened to Babe Ruth.
He ate two eggs
every single day,
and now he's dead,
so what else is there to say?

That sounds good
It's what we will do.
So serve them one egg,
never ever two.
One egg!
One egg!
No more!
It's because eggs will make you fat,
not because we're poor!

One egg!
One egg!
No more!

Kalani Ain't Kalani Anymore

Kalani ain't Kalani anymore.
Just leave your aloha at the door.
Come on in and take abuse.
You can try to fight it,
but there is no use.
Kalani ain't Kalani anymore.
Derrik's in charge,
that is why.
The Board of Directors appointed him,
but did they even interview this guy?
Where did he come from,
does anybody know?
He's threatened to kill us,
but the Board won't tell him to go.
He's not going anywhere
so we live in fear.
Is this how it ends,
because the end is here.
Kalani ain't Kalani anymore.

Derrik has a gun
and we have proof.
It's under his pillow
under our roof.
Why does he have it,
who's he going to shoot?
Why won't the board fire him,
give him the boot?
Who has to die
before they will see,
Derrik is a menace.
to Kalani
and the monkey pod tree.
He's belligerent
and he is rude.
Man oh man,

we can't stand that dude.
He's lazy
but expects us to work.
Jesus Christ,
that guy's a jerk.
"I'm here for the aina"
is all he'll say.
When asked his plan
for Kalani's new day.
What does that mean,
can anybody guess?
It means he wants the land
every tree
every building
every grain of sand.
Kalani ain't Kalani anymore.

He's not here for us,
only for himself.
His true colors show
and continue to grow
darker and darker,
then darker still.
He'll kick us all out
if we don't bend to his will.
"Don't let the gate hit you in the ass."
That's a true quote
from this Jackass.
"Fuck you if you if you decide to leave."
Now we see what is up his sleeve.
No aloha in words like that.
Now he's walking around with
a baseball bat,
threatening our lives
threatening our peace.
When will his reign of terror cease?
Kalani ain't Kalani anymore.

Where's the Board
why do they coddle to him?

Let's just hope that asshole can swim,
because it's time to matter into our own hands.
He can't have our souls
and he can't have our lands.
We're going to dump in the ocean
tied to his bed.
Because that's what happens
when power goes to your head.
Are you watching Board?
That's what we think.
When you put a psycho in charge
who needs a head shrink.
And now
Kalani ain't Kalani anymore.

Board of Directors,
just quit
just go away.
We don't need you,
we'll be okay.
Stop making decisions from so far away.
You don't know the situation
because you never come to stay.
You have your nice safe houses
away from the fear.
You stay far away
you never come near.
Kalani is dead
no thanks to you.
There is really nothing
more for you to do.
Kalani ain't Kalani anymore.

Kalani ain't Kalani anymore.
Derrik came
so we checked our aloha at the door.
We fought it
and we finally won.
We fought the devil
and we fought his son.

It was a hell of a battle,
and it still ain't done.

Kalani ain't Kalani anymore.
Kalani ain't Kalani anymore.
"Aloha."

Existential Crisis

What am I doing?
Why am I here
Oh dear.
Existential crisis.
La la la la la la.

Success

It at first you don't succeed, then there must be something seriously fucking wrong with you. Get your shit together. Seriously.

Give Me Wind

Give me wind so I can fly.
Otherwise, I fear I'll die.
And I don't want to die,
no not today.
I don't want to die,
no not this way.
I want to die having lived my life.
I don't want to die
from boredom and strife.

I need action
adventure
and fun.
I need to fly
too close to the sun.
I need to crash having tried.
In this way,
you can say I died.
Don't let me die
having never flown.
I don't want familiar
to be all I've known.

I need to know life's great
mystery.
I need to climb
Life's Master Tree.
To look around
and see what I see.

So give me wind
so I can try
to spread my wings
and fly
fly
fly.

The Anti-Christ

When we think of the anti-Christ, it is pretty normal to think of a horrible being bent on the destruction of human kind. And while the anti-Christ, in reality, isn't really that bad, he is something of a dick head.

So who is the ant-Christ really? The answer is summed up in his name. "Anti" meaning to go against. And "Christ" meaning Jesus. So the anti-Christ was somebody who went against Jesus. Essentially, the Anti-Christ was just a big bully who made life hard for Jesus when he was on the earth, always undermining his efforts to bring love and peace to the world.

What exactly did the anti-Christ look like, you may ask. I will tell you. The Anti-Christ looks like Jesus, only dirty. He has dreadlocks, but not cool looking dreadlocks. His dread locks look nasty and mangy. And he has tattoos all up and down both arms and one or two front teeth missing. He may or may not be wearing a shirt, but he always wears several necklaces of tiny little sea shells, aka "Puna Bling." If you see this person, he is the anti-Christ and while he won't hurt you, he may try to make you cry. He's been known to hang out at Kehena beach in the mid-morning most week days.

The Anti-Christ had it in for Jesus right from the start. As a child, Jesus was often heard to say, "When I grow up, I'm going to be a carpenter!" The anti-Christ, in an effort to undermine the young Christ Child's confidence would tell him, "You can't be a carpenter. You'll hit your thumb with a hammer." Fortunately for the young messiah, he had a strong father influence in his life to assure him he can grow up to be whatever he wanted to be.

The anti-Christ followed Jesus throughout his life, always criticizing, always undermining him, always trying to take away his glory. When Jesus performed the miracle of the bread, do you know what the anti-Christ did? He took away all the butter. While it was nice that they had bread to eat, it sucked that they had nothing to put on it. When Jesus made all the fish so they could feed the multitudes, the anti-Christ scooped a bunch of them up in buckets and threw them in the sea of Galilee. When Jesus rose the dead on the road to Damascus, The Anti-Christ went right behind him and convinced him he needed an expensive life insurance policy, saying , "What happens if Jesus isn't there the next time? What will your family do if you don't rise from the dead?" When Jesus walked across the water, the anti-Christ rowed next to him in a canoe, splashing him with the paddle, trying to make him fall. When Jesus turned the water into wine, the Anti-Christ shook the bottles so it would go flat right away. When Jesus was resurrected from the grave after the crucifixion, who do you think was holding the boulder on the other side of the cave entrance to make it difficult for him to get out? Yep. It was the anti-Christ.

They say Jesus is going to be back one day, and I believe it. The ant-Christ is already here waiting for him. Like I said, he hangs out down at Kehena beach with dreadlocks and puna bling around his neck. If you see him down there, just give him his space. You don't need any of his shit.

The Ballad of Jim Larsen

Born in the Valley of San Juaquin
He's the coolest dude we've ever seen.
Made his first movie when he was sixteen
Grew up among cedars
which are evergreen.
Jim! Jim Larsen. King of the cool people.

Raised in Virginia on the family farm
The girls all love him for his charm.
He has three tattoos on his right arm
He's a psychopath
but he he'll do you no harm.
Jim! Jim Larsen. The most incredible man alive.

Loved his first woman on a reservation
Stood tall and proud for the Sioux Indian Nation
Went to Montana for his matriculation
but partied too hard for his education.
Jim! Jim Larsen. A legend in his own time.

In 1998 Troma Films released Buttcrack
an epic film about a zombie attack
Jim wrote this movie and directed it too
Most people love it
How about you?
Jim! Jim Larsen. There's nobody more amazing than him!

Came to Kalani in 2007
Took one look around and said "This place is Heaven"
He liked it so much
and that is why
He bought himself a cottage at Kalani Kai.
Jim! Jim Larsen. You only wish you could be him.

Went off to China and met a girl named Fifi
She looked at him and said "Well, Tee hee hee.

That handsome American will be mine."
Jim looked at her
and said, "You'll do me just fine. "
Jim! Jim Larsen. He really doesn't care how young his girlfriends are.

Spends every evening in his bubble bath
all those bubbles really make him laugh
Little Rubber Ducky is his best friend
They'll stay together
until the end.
Jim! Jim Larsen. The October 2008 Volunteer of the Month!

Jim Larsen's heart's the biggest heart
His heart's the best.
Filters out bad people,
and let's in the rest.
He flosses every day
and brushes his teeth with Crest!
He's a gentleman,
so he won't stare at your breast.
Jim! Jim Larsen! The coolest dude you all know!
Jim! Jim Larsen! He'll go down in history!

Cha cha cha!

Refried

One time they fried the beans once, but it didn't take so they fried them again, and we had refried beans for lunch that day. That sort of thing would never happen if they would just fry potatoes instead.

English Muffin Boy

Sometimes in the morning at breakfast I'll be toasting an English Muffin and somebody will inevitably ask me if staring at the English Muffin makes it toast faster. That is in an example of what I call a Stupid Question." The answer is, of course, no. Of course not. That would suggest that I have the power to toast an English Muffin with just the power of my eyes, which is ridiculous. If I had that power, I wouldn't have to put the English Muffin in the toaster to begin with.

The more I think about it though, the more I wish I did have the power to toast an English Muffin with just the power of my eyes because that would fall under the category of "Super Power." And if I had super powers, then I could fulfill my life-long ambition of being a super villain, then I'd be famous and have a really cool back story, like I was betrayed early in life, or something like that, and now my thirst for revenge has gotten out of hand and I'm no longer in control of my evil deeds. My evil deeds are in control of me.

But as it is, my back story is pretty dull. I ain't nothing but the son of a dairy farmer who grew up on a farm in Virginia and had to ride 20 miles on a bus to get to school when I was a teenager. Whoop-dee-do.

But if I were a super villain, I would be on the front page of the paper pretty much everyday and my super villain name would be "English Muffin Boy" and the headlines would say things like, "English Muffin Boy Strikes Again!" and "City Paralyzed with Fear as English Muffin Boy Attacks!" and "Who is English Muffin Boy?" and "President Bush Calls for Vigilance in the Hunt for English Muffin Boy."

My costume would be awesome! It would have the letters "EMB" across my chest, which would stand for "English Muffin Boy." And then Spider Man would be trying to capture me, because when I said my back story was that I was betrayed early in life, it was Peter Parker who betrayed me and I know he is Spider Man.

That would be cool if Spider Man was trying to capture me because that way I could kidnap his girl friend, Mary Jane and cut off her Pinky Finger and send it to the Daily Planet, which I know is where Super Man works and not Spider Man, but once the story hits the AP wire, Spider Man will read it and become enraged and go after me, and an epic battle will ensue.

Oh yeah, and at the scene of every crime I will leave my calling card, which will be a toasted English Muffin with butter and jam on it. Sometimes it will be strawberry jam, and sometimes it will be raspberry jam, and sometimes it will be liliquoi jam, and sometimes it will be some other kind of jam, like blueberry jam. Forensic investigators will try to make sense of it, like, if the kind of jam I use is some kind of clue as to where I will strike next, but it won't be. The kind of jam I use really just depends on whatever I happen to be carrying in my man-purse at the time.

So yeah, an epic battle will ensue, and in the end, Spider Man will win, of course. The thing about being the super hero is that you always win out over the super villain, and I accept that. But the good thing about being a super villain is that you always get to break out of prison, just like Magneto from X-Men did.

So that is probably what will happen- Spider Man will catch me and I'll be thrown into Arkham Asylum, which is a Bat man thing, I know, but that's where I will end up and I'll make friends with The Riddler and we'll join forces and become the most feared evil duo the world has ever known and we'll bust out of Arkham and dominate the world from our under water fortress where Aqua Man, or better yet, Namor the Submariner, will try to stop us.

So yeah, does staring at an English muffin make it toast faster? Of course not. I wish you wouldn't waste my time with stupid questions like that.

Pushy

Sometimes, I push people out of my way. It is not necessarily that they are in my way, but really this is a style of yoga that I've developed. If you pay attention, you will notice that when I push you, I am breathing deeply and chanting Ohm.

Staring

Sometimes you may think that I am staring at you. It's not that I particularly want to look at you, it's just that there is something about you that I am confused by and I am trying to figure it out. Or maybe, it could be that there is something on the other side of you that I find interesting, and I am just waiting for you to move so I can get a good look at it.

Toast Love

I liken my love for thee to toast.

When I met you, you were completely beige and at room temperature. But then I turned up the heat of my love for you, now you're all hot and brown and a little burnt, for which I apologize, but that's the way I like you, because I love you, darling.

I liken my love for thee to toast, all smothered in the butter of my affection, seeping into all of your nooks and crannies and pores. MMM! You're sure gonna taste good. I can't wait to sink my teeth into you and start chewing. I'm going to crunch you up real good because that's what I like to do because I love you, darling.

I liken my love for thee to toast with a generous amount of starfruit and ginger jelly smeared all over you because that's how much I love you. But none of it is Smuckers. Uh-uh. No way. There ain't no love in a jar of Smuckers that compares to the love I have for you, because I love you. This jelly of my love is natural and organic and locally sourced, just like my love for you, darling.

I liken my love for thee to toast. I should probably eat you over a counter or the dining room table in case I drop you, which I'll try not to do, but I might because I love you. I'd hate for you to land on the floor jelly-side down. That would just make a mess I wouldn't know how to clean up, because I love you.

I liken my love for thee to toast. What do you liken your love for me to? I bet you liken your love for me to a bowl of Cap'n Crunch cereal, in a big old bowl with the milk of your desire poured all over me, because that's how much you love me, ain't that right, darling?

Seems like you love me just as much as I love you, so I will propose a marriage to you right now, because I liken my love for thee to toast, and I love toast, just like I love you, darling, so I offer you my hand. So, let's get married and then go live together, because I love you.

Son of Godzilla

The son of Godzilla, that would be Jesuszilla, right?

A Big Sign

It was one of those big maps, like ones they have in shopping malls or public parks. There was an arrow on it that pointed away. It said, "You are over there." So I went over there, and when I got there, sure enough- there I was. That's when I realized, there is something going on that is so much bigger than any of us can know, and I'm going to figure it out.

Zombie Dream

Last night I dreamed I was watching a documentary about zombie films and they mentioned a new breed of zombies as represented in the film, "Bullet Proof Zombies." They showed a clip of this movie, and it was very intense. It was animated and had the overall look of a video game. These zombies were moving at incredible speeds, crashing through the fences of a suburban neighborhood and ripping people apart with copious amounts of very red blood everywhere. Then I woke up and noticed my girlfriend had started her period.

Disconcerting

Sometimes it can be disconcerting to want peace and quiet, but what you get instead is a mildly retarded massage therapist making chicken noises at a screaming child.

Miracles

On a scale of miracles, if Jesus turning water into wine is a 10, then I guess my ability to soften a butter packet with Reiki energy is probably a 4.

Understanding

People try to figure me out. It is fun watch. They search for words based on their own understandings, but they come up short. They don't have the vocabulary or the point of reference necessary to comprehend the full reality of the me that is before them. I appreciate that they try, but a lot of the time, they just get on my nerves.

Kaunakakai

My, my, my, Kaunakakai
home of the midnight bread.
The fish is
delicious
and everybody is always well fed.

My, my, my, Kaunakakai.
Kaunakakai, Kaunakakai
here on the island of Molokai.
Wonder why I love Kaunakakai?
I'll tell you what I spy
with my eye
from my back porch
in Kaunakakai.

Across the ocean I see
Maui, Lanai, and even the Big I
All right here from Kaunakakai.

The friendliness of the people
may drive you crazy
if you're used to people who
are rude, crude and crazy.

So do your best
and try to adjust
to all that friendliness
and trust
trust
trust.

The the people are real
they are not phony.
Hang out at the coffee shop,
you'll never be lonely.

This is life
in Kaunakakai.
Give it a shot
and you'll see why,
I sure do love
Kaunakakai.

Kaunakakai
Kaunakakai.
Right here
on the island of Molokai.

Hugs

I wonder how many people are like me when hugging. That's the problem. If I'm hugging somebody, I can't see their face, so I don't know if they are rolling their eyes and making weird faces. It is probably a safe bet that they are, so that's what I do too just to get back at them for doing that to me. My affection will not be mocked!

How to Listen

Somebody with a lot of patience needs to be the listener for these people. If nobody is listening, then they are just talking to themselves, and so few people are comfortable doing that. They have this acute need to focus their words towards somebody. When these people are talking at you, you don't even have to listen for real. I know I never do. Just provide them with the sense that you care about what they are saying, and they'll be happy. Every so often say something like "really?" and "Hmm. Interesting" It's also helpful to know when to say "I never really thought of that" or "That's true, isn't it?" You got to nod your head every now and then. Nodding your head sends the talker the signal that "I'm listening and I'm interested" even if you're not either one. Make as much eye contact as you can stand, but try not to stare. These are the skills you develop as you go along in life. You'll go crazy if you don't.

Christianity

Maybe Christianity has placed a set of responsibilities on Jesus that he would not have otherwise had. Maybe he was looking forward to retirement in the afterlife, but then mankind went and created a religion in his name, so now he feels like he has to live up to it and stay busy all the time. Christians are selfish.

Blah Blah Blah

People talk. They talk a lot. I see people sometimes, and all they are doing is talking. I look at the person they are talking to, and it is unimaginable what they must be going through having to listen to all that. Blah blah blah. It's not even what I would call a conversation, what's going on. I love conversations. Just make sure that's what's going on when you start talking to me. One of the worst things in the world is feeling like a hostage, trapped in a cage with words being thrown at me. I hate that like you don't even know. So make sure that I want to hear what you have to say, and then give me a chance to say something back at you that is pertinent and relevant. And then you do the same. Let's do that a few times over and over. And then bam! We're having a conversation. The minute you start prattling on about how cute some kitten is though, I'm going to walk as far as I can away from you. Either that or I'm going to put you on a raft and shove you out into the ocean because nobody should have to listen to that. I can see for myself how cute a kitten is. So naturally, I'm confused. What exactly are you expecting from me? What do you want? Is this one of those grabs for validation? You need me to make you feel good that you have a sense of what cute is? You don't need me for that. You can get that from anybody. And honestly, that's not even that cute of a kitten. Kind of ugly, actually. You think that's a cute kitten? You need to go back to school, because you don't know nothing.

Salad Dressing

Something we do once a week in the kitchen is clean out the reach in refrigerator and throw out all the leftovers that are over a week old. I love it when it's my turn to do that job, because I refuse to let anything go to waste. What I will do is, I'll take all the leftovers, run them through the blender, add some vinegar and serve it as a salad dressing. I'll come up with some fancy name for it like, "Raspberry Vinaigrette." I say this just so you know what you are putting on your salad when you go for the raspberry vinaigrette. You have a right to know.

Teacher of So Much

One time I was teaching an English lesson to adults in China. At the end of the classs, I asked, "So, are there any questions?" One of the women in the class said. "Mmm, teacher. Can I ask you. When is it normal to kiss good night? For example… there was a dark skin man. He was, I think,from South Africa. We eat together… we go to restaurant only four times and he say he want to kiss me goodnight. Why? Why so? Is this okay to do? I only know him… I only see him four times and I don't know why he want to kiss me goodnight. Why so? Teacher, I am… I am not comfortable to kiss him goodnight. Is this how it is in your country? Do you kiss goodnight? When? When do you kiss goodnight? When you first meet? Or do kiss goodnight if you become a partner with them? When do you kiss good-night because I am not comfortable to have this man do that. Teacher.I do not understand. Why?" I knew this was an important issue for this girl, and I really did want to give a compassionate and honest answer. I tell her what I think is the right thing to tell her and what she most needs to hear and understand and then I ask my original question again, this time phrasing it more carefully than before based on the lesson we had just finished. "So, are there any questions… about using adjectives to describe the weather?" On paper, I was an English teacher. In reality though, I taught so much more.

Old School Kalani Kitchen

On April 11 of this year at precisely eighteen hundred hours I heard the conch blown the worst I have ever heard it blown in my entire history at Kalani. It was such a horrible sound that it brought tears of pain to my eyes and bricks of terror to my gut. When it happened, I was resting in the hammock beneath the autograph tree, my mind drifting to wherever it goes when it drifts. I was wrenched from my meditation by a sound so horrible that human words are inadequate to describe it. I bolted from the hammock fearful and so awfully afraid that that catastrophe and peril were imminent. But then I heard it again. And again. That's when the sickening truth hit me. Oh my God. That's the conch.

Of course, I had to know who it was that was blowing it, so I looked. But I will not say. It is not my ambition to call anybody out or cause embarrassment, but I will say this. I really admired this person. Here is somebody able and adept at putting his pride on the line to risk the taunts and laughter of his ohana, Kalani guests, and visitors from the outside, as well as any Hawaiian dignitaries who may be on the lanai on official business. I hereby applaud this person, for he reminds me of myself in my early days of Kalani volunteer service, as I myself began in the kitchen. Even though the first time I sounded the conch, I did it pitch perfect, I had my own humiliations and problems to work through in that department.

You see, back in my day working in the kitchen, we blew the conch for one reason and one reason only. We blew it to mark the beginning of meal time. And that was it. Nobody applauded us and nobody said "woo-hoo" and we didn't care. We weren't putting on a show for anybody, and we didn't need validation. We blew the conch to announce meal times. Period. And another thing, we didn't practice blowing the conch in the walk in refrigerator either. We went out on the lanai with the conch and we blew it for the first time right there in front of the ohana, the guests, and God himself. If we made the sound of a dying whale, we sucked it up and tried again. Yes, all eyes were on us, and they were hungry eyes. With the pinpricks of judgment baring into us, we knew if we didn't find the fortitude to get it right, we would forever be branded "conch sucker" and rightfully so, because we did suck at blowing the conch. We weren't coddled to, and we didn't ask for special treatment. We dug deep into our souls to find the power, and those that found it went on to thrive in the kitchen. Those that didn't were classified as weak and spent most of their time emptying the slop buckets and bussing dishes from tables. Yeah. Welcome to Heaven on Earth, conch sucker.

It was a different era in the kitchen. This was a time when calling out "Hot Pan!" or "Sharp Knife!" wasn't done as a cautionary statement, but rather as a warning out of pitiless anger vented at somebody frequently followed by the words, "muthafucker."I wonder how many of the current kitchen staff would have been able to handle the old school kitchen. I really do. I think every one of them would have gone home crying to their mommas, shaking and trembling, needing a hug a soothing word or two. "It's okay, no hot pans here. No hot pans."

Let me tell you about my first kitchen shift. On my first shift in the kitchen, the shift leader looked me square in the eye and said "You're just a volunteer. Not much is expected of you. You're going to make a lot of mistakes." That was it. Welcome to the kitchen, Jim. Good luck. "You're going to make a lot of mistakes." I went ahead and let that set the tone for the year to come.

In those days, we didn't have "trainers" and we didn't need them and we didn't want them. You know who your trainer was? It was the person standing next to you, and you had to pray they had a minute to tell you anything at all about what you're supposed to be doing. Otherwise, good luck figuring it out on your own. Just watch what the others do and do what they're doing. That's how you found your place in the kitchen. But if they are chopping carrots, guess what? Somebody is already chopping carrots, so go find something else to do. Go wash the dishes. But guess what? Somebody is already washing the dishes. So what are you going to do now? You better find something fast because here comes the shift leader. "What are doing? Why aren't you working? What is your major malfunction?"
"I don't know. I don't know."

"Ah Christ. Just empty the slop buckets, maggot."

Great. Now you're known as the conch-sucking slop bucket guy. Good luck getting past that, loser.

In those days, there wasn't a designated person whose job it was to make salad dressing. You know whose job it was to make salad dressing? Whoever wasn't busy doing something else at the moment the need for more salad dressing was discovered. That's why I would always want to look busy doing something else when the salad dressing was low, otherwise I would get stuck doing it and I hated it. Sometimes I would just walk around the kitchen with a dirty plate in my hand just to look like I was in the middle of something else. Anything to avoid having to make salad dressing.

I got stuck making the salad dressing once. Only once. After that, I was banned from ever making it again. I guess it didn't turn out too good. I don't know. I didn't try it. I saw how it was made.

I don't remember anymore what kind it was, but the recipe called for buttermilk. Is buttermilk even something we carry in the kitchen? Because if it is, I sure couldn't find it. But by now I was too far into making this recipe to turn back. Buttermilk or no buttermilk, I had to continue on. The Ohana is counting on me.

I asked myself, what exactly is buttermilk? The answer is in the name itself. You got butter. You got milk. Now whip the two together. So I grabbed a handful of those little butter packets and a carton of milk. In my mind, this made sense, as long as I didn't have to explain it to anybody. But it's hard to unwrap thirty or so little butter packets into a blender full of milk in a crowded and busy kitchen without somebody asking why you are doing that. And these are savvy people. You really can't bullshit your away around it when they say "What the hell are you doing?" Which is exactly what I got asked.

Now, I was faced with two choices. I could either play dumb like I didn't know any better than to do this, or I could play like my superr intelligence was beyond their capacity to comprehend when it comes to my culinary brilliance concocting a gourmet salad dressing to tantalize and delight their puny taste buds in a way they have never and will never experience again. I'm not sure which of these options I took. "I'm making buttermilk… for a salad dressing. I grew up on a farm. This is how we did it." That's always been my pat answer when I don't know how to explain myself. "I grew up on a farm" as if that alone will explain away all my peculiarities. "I grew up on a farm. Everybody dances this way where I'm from." "I grew up on a farm. This is how I learned to kiss a girl." Or "I grew up on a farm. This is how I was taught to hold a spoon."

This either worked and he was convinced of my genius, or he saw the futility of arguing with me, but he walked away to go do something else leaving me alone to figure out a suitable way to improvise the mustard seed that the recipe also called for, but the kitchen didn't have any of either. Hmm, where do we keep those little mustard packs we put in the bag lunches? If I mix those with chia seeds…

After that, I was pretty much left alone to do whatever I wanted in the kitchen, and if nothing was expected of me before, even less than nothing was expected of me now. Eventually I became the front of house person. As you may imagine, I had a lot fun making creative teas and juices for all to refresh their thirsty selves with. That didn't last too long though. Eventually I moved to what was then the "Landscaping" department where I really found myself as I connected with the aina here.

Time has a way of going on and changing everything in its path. Eventually the entire kitchen management and operations was overhauled and morphed into what it is today. Some of what I see, I think is good, and some of what I see I think is bad. I still don't agree with vegetarian Sundays. I think that is the worst idea anybody ever had here at Kalani, although that eggplant Parmesan we had a couple Sundays ago was awesome. So if the conch blower that night had to go practice in the walk in as not to be branded a conch sucker before they served it, I guess I will just have to be okay with that.

Landscaping is Better than the Kitchen

After spending an accumulative one year in the Kalani kitchen, I decided I don't like it there. I really really really really really really really hate it. I think it is a very very very very very very bad place to work. It is the most unhappy department at Kalani, and everybody knows it. It is a true fact that it has the highest suicide rate of all the departments at Kalani, and I couldn't wait to get out of there. Every shift I worked, morning or afternoon, was pure, undeniable Hell. There were so many times when I almost, picked up one of those large carving knives and went back into the walk in and slit my wrists.

But something always made me reconsider. Something always gave me hope for a happier and more fruitful tomorrow. Even in my darkest hour, there was one thing- one thing that kept me alive, and that thing was the sight of the landscaping crew and what a good time that they were having and the hope that maybe someday I could join them, and you know what? One day I did join them, and it was like being reborn into a universe of joy. If you don't believe me that the Landscaping department is better than the kitchen, listen as I tell you of a typical week in Landscaping. Mondays are awesome. We have our meeting and then we spend an hour or something chanting or whatever, then Barcus tells us where he wants us to pull weeds and we'll go pull a few of weeds or whatever, and then we pass a pint of Jim Beam or Jack Daniels around, or whatever, by the pool and talk about stuff or whatever and wait for Kimo to pick us up and take us down for ice cream on Barcus's tab. Meanwhile in the kitchen, another volunteer just took out the pig slop and never came back. His body, of course, will eventually be found in the jungle with a note pinned to it saying "The kitchen did this to me."

Tuesdays are kind of the same, except we might have races on the riding lawnmowers. I don't know why. The Craftsman always wins, but we keep racing it against the Kubodo anyway. Then we'll pull a couple of weeds or whatever and smoke some doobies by the pool and wait for Kimo to pick us up and take us down for some ice cream. Meanwhile, at Kehena Beach, the body of the latest kitchen victim has washed up on shore. Her final words before surrendering to the great abyss were, "I ain't doing the Hobart no more. I ain't doing the Hobart… no more."

Wednesdays are a little different. On Wednesdays we work on the orchard, which is close to where Michael Salita lives. Working in the orchard is fun because Barcus tells us what trees he wants us to cut down, but then as soon as he goes to the office to check his email, we eat some magic mushrooms and play with the chainsaws and just cut down whatever trees we want until Kimo shows up and takes us down for ice cream. Meanwhile in the kitchen, a knife fight has broken out, again, between two volunteers over whose going to do the dishes and who's going to prep the lettuce for the salad bar. This happens all the time and the shift leaders are all a bunch of wusses who just stand back and let it happen until it's time to mop the blood up off the floor, then suddenly it's a big issue.

Then on Thursday, that's the best day because we are back in the orchard where we start a fire and have a sing along to our favorite songs by Night Ranger. Sometimes we sing "Sister Christian" but then sometimes we sing "Sentimental Street." Really, we just sing along to whatever Night Ranger song we want to. We don't always sing along to Night Ranger though. Sometimes we sing along to John Cafferty and the Beaver Brown Band. My favorite song by them is "On The Dark Side" from the movie Eddie and the Cruisers. Then, we sneak off and have sexual relations with one another until Kimo shows up and takes us down for ice cream. And that's pretty much what we do in Landscaping. It's much, much better than the kitchen where all they ever do is chop onions and drag the mats out. So, if you're really sick of the kitchen, come join us in Landscaping. You do have a choice. You don't have to kill yourself.

Prosthetic Hand

One time, I saw somebody walking my direction and thought she had a prosthetic hand, and thought, that's pretty cool, but I better not get caught staring at her. But then she got closer to me and I saw her hand was normal; she was just carrying a fork. I didn't feel so bad about staring at her after that.

Chainsaw Boy Strikes Again

We invited you back, and what did you do?
You pissed the neighbors off,
and now they might sue.
Will they sue us?
No, they'll sue you.
Chainsaw Boy strikes again.

The trees across the road
grow on State Land.
That seems to be something
you don't understand.
When you cut them down,
the neighbors get upset.
Don't even question it,
it's a sure bet.
Think we'll protect you?
Better think again.
We're not your babysitters
so face up to your sin.
Chainsaw Boy
just go home and don't come back.
We are really, really weary
from your absence of tact.

You do stupid things
and then try to hide.
No longer will we protect you,
believe me,
we tried.
You apologize, and beg forgiveness
and we believe you are true.
But next thing you know,
what do you do?

You go back
to your really stupid ways

I swear to Good,
you're head is stuck in a haze.
of meth, of pot,
and I'm sure a lot more.
You were never that fun
and now you're just a bore.

When the officials come
and say "Where's that Chainsaw Boy?
Can you do us a favor,
and confiscate his toy?
Chainsaws are meant for grownup use.
Not for over grown man-children
running around on the loose."
Chainsaw Boy,
please tell us what you expect us to do.
This is your problem,
it's all up to you.

We can't cover you,
no, not forever.
Sorry, none of us
are quite that clever,
to make an excuse week after week
for your behavior
and the attention you seek.
So when you piss the neighbors off
and the State Officials too,
because you cut state trees down
to get a better view.
We'll say,
"That's him.
That's him right there."
Chainsaw Boy,
we're not going
to protect your derriere.
Remember that,
Chainsaw Boy.
If you're going to go rouge,
with our chainsaw in your hand,

you're not marching to your own drummer,
you got your own band.
Your actions are not pono
by any sense of the word.
You're not Hawaiian cool,
you're a haole nerd
who can't seem to get it in his head,
you can't do something wrong,
and then hide under your bed.

Enough is enough
and when things get rough
having you around,
makes it even rougher,
and then times get tougher.
It seems like
when you're here,
all we do is suffer.

I don't need to suffer,
no not anymore,
so Chainsaw Boy,
let yourself out the door.
Leave the saw here,
and just go home.

Chainsaw Boy Strikes again

GLAND
CONDITION

Also by Jim Larsen

Fat Naked Poetry

The Pieces of You Tarot: Illuminating the Archetypes Within

What's Tarot Got to do With It?: The Fool's Path to
Enlightnement

The Double Oh Fool Guide to Tarot Mastery

Knowings from The Silence: Simple Wisdom for an Enlight-
ened Life vvols. 1-4

www.ingramcontent.com/pod-product-compliance
Lightning Source LLC
Chambersburg PA
CBHW060712030426
42337CB00017B/2844